This book belongs to:

____

Date:

____

Website:

Username: Email:

Password:

Security Question 1:

Security Answer 1:

Security Question 2:

Security Answer 2:

Notes:

Website:

Username: Email:

Password:

Security Question 1:

Security Answer 1:

Security Question 2:

Security Answer 2:

Notes:

Website:

Username: Email:

Password:

Security Question 1:

Security Answer 1:

Security Question 2:

Security Answer 2:

Notes:

Website:

Username: Email:

Password:

Security Question 1:

Security Answer 1:

Security Question 2:

Security Answer 2:

Notes:

Website:

Username: Email:

Password:

Security Question 1:

Security Answer 1:

Security Question 2:

Security Answer 2:

Notes:

Website:

Username: Email:

Password:

Security Question 1:

Security Answer 1:

Security Question 2:

Security Answer 2:

Notes:

Website:

Username: Email:

Password:

Security Question 1:

Security Answer 1:

Security Question 2:

Security Answer 2:

Notes:

Website:

Username: Email:

Password:

Security Question 1:

Security Answer 1:

Security Question 2:

Security Answer 2:

Notes:

Website:

Username: Email:

Password:

Security Question 1:

Security Answer 1:

Security Question 2:

Security Answer 2:

Notes:

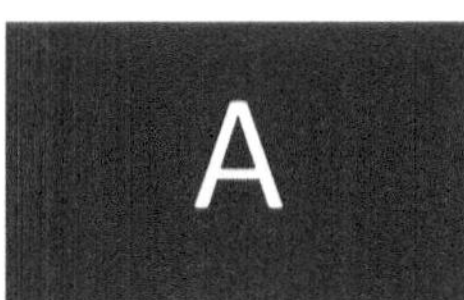

Website:

Username: Email:

Password:

Security Question 1:

Security Answer 1:

Security Question 2:

Security Answer 2:

Notes:

Website:

Username: Email:

Password:

Security Question 1:

Security Answer 1:

Security Question 2:

Security Answer 2:

Notes:

Website:

Username: Email:

Password:

Security Question 1:

Security Answer 1:

Security Question 2:

Security Answer 2:

Notes:

Website:

Username: Email:

Password:

Security Question 1:

Security Answer 1:

Security Question 2:

Security Answer 2:

Notes:

Website:

Username: Email:

Password:

Security Question 1:

Security Answer 1:

Security Question 2:

Security Answer 2:

Notes:

Website:

Username: Email:

Password:

Security Question 1:

Security Answer 1:

Security Question 2:

Security Answer 2:

Notes:

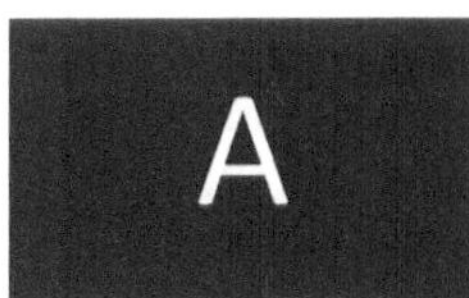

Website:

Username: Email:

Password:

Security Question 1:

Security Answer 1:

Security Question 2:

Security Answer 2:

Notes:

Website:

Username: Email:

Password:

Security Question 1:

Security Answer 1:

Security Question 2:

Security Answer 2:

Notes:

Website:

Username: Email:

Password:

Security Question 1:

Security Answer 1:

Security Question 2:

Security Answer 2:

Notes:

B

Website:

Username: Email:

Password:

Security Question 1:

Security Answer 1:

Security Question 2:

Security Answer 2:

Notes:

Website:

Username: Email:

Password:

Security Question 1:

Security Answer 1:

Security Question 2:

Security Answer 2:

Notes:

Website:

Username: Email:

Password:

Security Question 1:

Security Answer 1:

Security Question 2:

Security Answer 2:

Notes:

B

Website:

Username: Email:

Password:

Security Question 1:

Security Answer 1:

Security Question 2:

Security Answer 2:

Notes:

Website:

Username: Email:

Password:

Security Question 1:

Security Answer 1:

Security Question 2:

Security Answer 2:

Notes:

Website:

Username: Email:

Password:

Security Question 1:

Security Answer 1:

Security Question 2:

Security Answer 2:

Notes:

B

Username: Email:

Password:

Security Question 1:

Security Answer 1:

Security Question 2:

Security Answer 2:

Notes:

Website:

Username: Email:

Password:

Security Question 1:

Security Answer 1:

Security Question 2:

Security Answer 2:

Notes:

Website:

Username: Email:

Password:

Security Question 1:

Security Answer 1:

Security Question 2:

Security Answer 2:

Notes:

Website:

Username: Email:

Password:

Security Question 1:

Security Answer 1:

Security Question 2:

Security Answer 2:

Notes:

Website:

Username: Email:

Password:

Security Question 1:

Security Answer 1:

Security Question 2:

Security Answer 2:

Notes:

Website:

Username: Email:

Password:

Security Question 1:

Security Answer 1:

Security Question 2:

Security Answer 2:

Notes:

Website:

Username: Email:

Password:

Security Question 1:

Security Answer 1:

Security Question 2:

Security Answer 2:

Notes:

Website:

Username: Email:

Password:

Security Question 1:

Security Answer 1:

Security Question 2:

Security Answer 2:

Notes:

Website:

Username: Email:

Password:

Security Question 1:

Security Answer 1:

Security Question 2:

Security Answer 2:

Notes:

B

Website:

Username: Email:

Password:

Security Question 1:

Security Answer 1:

Security Question 2:

Security Answer 2:

Notes:

Website:

Username: Email:

Password:

Security Question 1:

Security Answer 1:

Security Question 2:

Security Answer 2:

Notes:

Website:

Username: Email:

Password:

Security Question 1:

Security Answer 1:

Security Question 2:

Security Answer 2:

Notes:

Website:

Username: Email:

Password:

Security Question 1:

Security Answer 1:

Security Question 2:

Security Answer 2:

Notes:

Website:

Username: Email:

Password:

Security Question 1:

Security Answer 1:

Security Question 2:

Security Answer 2:

Notes:

Website:

Username: Email:

Password:

Security Question 1:

Security Answer 1:

Security Question 2:

Security Answer 2:

Notes:

C

Website:

Username: Email:

Password:

Security Question 1:

Security Answer 1:

Security Question 2:

Security Answer 2:

Notes:

Website:

Username: Email:

Password:

Security Question 1:

Security Answer 1:

Security Question 2:

Security Answer 2:

Notes:

Website:

Username: Email:

Password:

Security Question 1:

Security Answer 1:

Security Question 2:

Security Answer 2:

Notes:

Website:

Username: Email:

Password:

Security Question 1:

Security Answer 1:

Security Question 2:

Security Answer 2:

Notes:

Website:

Username: Email:

Password:

Security Question 1:

Security Answer 1:

Security Question 2:

Security Answer 2:

Notes:

Website:

Username: Email:

Password:

Security Question 1:

Security Answer 1:

Security Question 2:

Security Answer 2:

Notes:

Website:

Username: Email:

Password:

Security Question 1:

Security Answer 1:

Security Question 2:

Security Answer 2:

Notes:

Website:

Username: Email:

Password:

Security Question 1:

Security Answer 1:

Security Question 2:

Security Answer 2:

Notes:

Website:

Username: Email:

Password:

Security Question 1:

Security Answer 1:

Security Question 2:

Security Answer 2:

Notes:

Website:

Username: Email:

Password:

Security Question 1:

Security Answer 1:

Security Question 2:

Security Answer 2:

Notes:

Website:

Username: Email:

Password:

Security Question 1:

Security Answer 1:

Security Question 2:

Security Answer 2:

Notes:

Website:

Username: Email:

Password:

Security Question 1:

Security Answer 1:

Security Question 2:

Security Answer 2:

Notes:

Website:

Username: Email:

Password:

Security Question 1:

Security Answer 1:

Security Question 2:

Security Answer 2:

Notes:

Website:

Username: Email:

Password:

Security Question 1:

Security Answer 1:

Security Question 2:

Security Answer 2:

Notes:

Website:

Username: Email:

Password:

Security Question 1:

Security Answer 1:

Security Question 2:

Security Answer 2:

Notes:

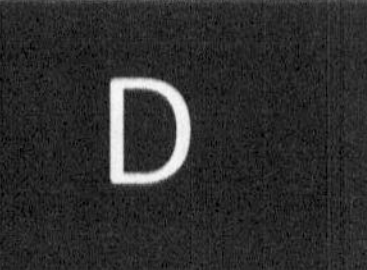

Website:

Username: | Email:

Password:

Security Question 1:

Security Answer 1:

Security Question 2:

Security Answer 2:

Notes:

Website:

Username: | Email:

Password:

Security Question 1:

Security Answer 1:

Security Question 2:

Security Answer 2:

Notes:

Website:

Username: | Email:

Password:

Security Question 1:

Security Answer 1:

Security Question 2:

Security Answer 2:

Notes:

Website:

Username: Email:

Password:

Security Question 1:

Security Answer 1:

Security Question 2:

Security Answer 2:

Notes:

Website:

Username: Email:

Password:

Security Question 1:

Security Answer 1:

Security Question 2:

Security Answer 2:

Notes:

Website:

Username: Email:

Password:

Security Question 1:

Security Answer 1:

Security Question 2:

Security Answer 2:

Notes:

Website:

Username: | Email:

Password:

Security Question 1:

Security Answer 1:

Security Question 2:

Security Answer 2:

Notes:

Website:

Username: | Email:

Password:

Security Question 1:

Security Answer 1:

Security Question 2:

Security Answer 2:

Notes:

Website:

Username: | Email:

Password:

Security Question 1:

Security Answer 1:

Security Question 2:

Security Answer 2:

Notes:

Website:

Username: Email:

Password:

Security Question 1:

Security Answer 1:

Security Question 2:

Security Answer 2:

Notes:

Website:

Username: Email:

Password:

Security Question 1:

Security Answer 1:

Security Question 2:

Security Answer 2:

Notes:

Website:

Username: Email:

Password:

Security Question 1:

Security Answer 1:

Security Question 2:

Security Answer 2:

Notes:

Website:

Username: Email:

Password:

Security Question 1:

Security Answer 1:

Security Question 2:

Security Answer 2:

Notes:

Website:

Username: Email:

Password:

Security Question 1:

Security Answer 1:

Security Question 2:

Security Answer 2:

Notes:

Website:

Username: Email:

Password:

Security Question 1:

Security Answer 1:

Security Question 2:

Security Answer 2:

Notes:

Website:

Username: Email:

Password:

Security Question 1:

Security Answer 1:

Security Question 2:

Security Answer 2:

Notes:

Website:

Username: Email:

Password:

Security Question 1:

Security Answer 1:

Security Question 2:

Security Answer 2:

Notes:

Website:

Username: Email:

Password:

Security Question 1:

Security Answer 1:

Security Question 2:

Security Answer 2:

Notes:

Website:

Username: Email:

Password:

Security Question 1:

Security Answer 1:

Security Question 2:

Security Answer 2:

Notes:

Website:

Username: Email:

Password:

Security Question 1:

Security Answer 1:

Security Question 2:

Security Answer 2:

Notes:

Website:

Username: Email:

Password:

Security Question 1:

Security Answer 1:

Security Question 2:

Security Answer 2:

Notes:

Website:

Username: Email:

Password:

Security Question 1:

Security Answer 1:

Security Question 2:

Security Answer 2:

Notes:

Website:

Username: Email:

Password:

Security Question 1:

Security Answer 1:

Security Question 2:

Security Answer 2:

Notes:

Website:

Username: Email:

Password:

Security Question 1:

Security Answer 1:

Security Question 2:

Security Answer 2:

Notes:

Website:

Username: Email:

Password:

Security Question 1:

Security Answer 1:

Security Question 2:

Security Answer 2:

Notes:

Website:

Username: Email:

Password:

Security Question 1:

Security Answer 1:

Security Question 2:

Security Answer 2:

Notes:

Website:

Username: Email:

Password:

Security Question 1:

Security Answer 1:

Security Question 2:

Security Answer 2:

Notes:

Website:

Username: Email:

Password:

Security Question 1:

Security Answer 1:

Security Question 2:

Security Answer 2:

Notes:

Website:

Username: Email:

Password:

Security Question 1:

Security Answer 1:

Security Question 2:

Security Answer 2:

Notes:

Website:

Username: Email:

Password:

Security Question 1:

Security Answer 1:

Security Question 2:

Security Answer 2:

Notes:

E

Website:

Username: Email:

Password:

Security Question 1:

Security Answer 1:

Security Question 2:

Security Answer 2:

Notes:

Website:

Username: Email:

Password:

Security Question 1:

Security Answer 1:

Security Question 2:

Security Answer 2:

Notes:

Website:

Username: Email:

Password:

Security Question 1:

Security Answer 1:

Security Question 2:

Security Answer 2:

Notes:

E

Website:

Username: Email:

Password:

Security Question 1:

Security Answer 1:

Security Question 2:

Security Answer 2:

Notes:

Website:

Username: Email:

Password:

Security Question 1:

Security Answer 1:

Security Question 2:

Security Answer 2:

Notes:

Website:

Username: Email:

Password:

Security Question 1:

Security Answer 1:

Security Question 2:

Security Answer 2:

Notes:

Website:

Username: Email:

Password:

Security Question 1:

Security Answer 1:

Security Question 2:

Security Answer 2:

Notes:

Website:

Username: Email:

Password:

Security Question 1:

Security Answer 1:

Security Question 2:

Security Answer 2:

Notes:

Website:

Username: Email:

Password:

Security Question 1:

Security Answer 1:

Security Question 2:

Security Answer 2:

Notes:

F

Website:

Username: Email:

Password:

Security Question 1:

Security Answer 1:

Security Question 2:

Security Answer 2:

Notes:

Website:

Username: Email:

Password:

Security Question 1:

Security Answer 1:

Security Question 2:

Security Answer 2:

Notes:

Website:

Username: Email:

Password:

Security Question 1:

Security Answer 1:

Security Question 2:

Security Answer 2:

Notes:

Website:

Username: Email:

Password:

Security Question 1:

Security Answer 1:

Security Question 2:

Security Answer 2:

Notes:

Website:

Username: Email:

Password:

Security Question 1:

Security Answer 1:

Security Question 2:

Security Answer 2:

Notes:

Website:

Username: Email:

Password:

Security Question 1:

Security Answer 1:

Security Question 2:

Security Answer 2:

Notes:

F

Website:

Username: Email:

Password:

Security Question 1:

Security Answer 1:

Security Question 2:

Security Answer 2:

Notes:

Website:

Username: Email:

Password:

Security Question 1:

Security Answer 1:

Security Question 2:

Security Answer 2:

Notes:

Website:

Username: Email:

Password:

Security Question 1:

Security Answer 1:

Security Question 2:

Security Answer 2:

Notes:

Website:

Username: Email:

Password:

Security Question 1:

Security Answer 1:

Security Question 2:

Security Answer 2:

Notes:

Website:

Username: Email:

Password:

Security Question 1:

Security Answer 1:

Security Question 2:

Security Answer 2:

Notes:

Website:

Username: Email:

Password:

Security Question 1:

Security Answer 1:

Security Question 2:

Security Answer 2:

Notes:

Website:

Username: Email:

Password:

Security Question 1:

Security Answer 1:

Security Question 2:

Security Answer 2:

Notes:

Website:

Username: Email:

Password:

Security Question 1:

Security Answer 1:

Security Question 2:

Security Answer 2:

Notes:

Website:

Username: Email:

Password:

Security Question 1:

Security Answer 1:

Security Question 2:

Security Answer 2:

Notes:

G

Website:

Username: Email:

Password:

Security Question 1:

Security Answer 1:

Security Question 2:

Security Answer 2:

Notes:

Website:

Username: Email:

Password:

Security Question 1:

Security Answer 1:

Security Question 2:

Security Answer 2:

Notes:

Website:

Username: Email:

Password:

Security Question 1:

Security Answer 1:

Security Question 2:

Security Answer 2:

Notes:

G

Website:

Username: Email:

Password:

Security Question 1:

Security Answer 1:

Security Question 2:

Security Answer 2:

Notes:

Website:

Username: Email:

Password:

Security Question 1:

Security Answer 1:

Security Question 2:

Security Answer 2:

Notes:

Website:

Username: Email:

Password:

Security Question 1:

Security Answer 1:

Security Question 2:

Security Answer 2:

Notes:

Website:

Username: Email:

Password:

Security Question 1:

Security Answer 1:

Security Question 2:

Security Answer 2:

Notes:

Website:

Username: Email:

Password:

Security Question 1:

Security Answer 1:

Security Question 2:

Security Answer 2:

Notes:

Website:

Username: Email:

Password:

Security Question 1:

Security Answer 1:

Security Question 2:

Security Answer 2:

Notes:

G

Website:

Username: Email:

Password:

Security Question 1:

Security Answer 1:

Security Question 2:

Security Answer 2:

Notes:

Website:

Username: Email:

Password:

Security Question 1:

Security Answer 1:

Security Question 2:

Security Answer 2:

Notes:

Website:

Username: Email:

Password:

Security Question 1:

Security Answer 1:

Security Question 2:

Security Answer 2:

Notes:

Website:

Username: Email:

Password:

Security Question 1:

Security Answer 1:

Security Question 2:

Security Answer 2:

Notes:

Website:

Username: Email:

Password:

Security Question 1:

Security Answer 1:

Security Question 2:

Security Answer 2:

Notes:

Website:

Username: Email:

Password:

Security Question 1:

Security Answer 1:

Security Question 2:

Security Answer 2:

Notes:

G

Website:

Username: Email:

Password:

Security Question 1:

Security Answer 1:

Security Question 2:

Security Answer 2:

Notes:

Website:

Username: Email:

Password:

Security Question 1:

Security Answer 1:

Security Question 2:

Security Answer 2:

Notes:

Website:

Username: Email:

Password:

Security Question 1:

Security Answer 1:

Security Question 2:

Security Answer 2:

Notes:

Website:

Username: Email:

Password:

Security Question 1:

Security Answer 1:

Security Question 2:

Security Answer 2:

Notes:

Website:

Username: Email:

Password:

Security Question 1:

Security Answer 1:

Security Question 2:

Security Answer 2:

Notes:

Website:

Username: Email:

Password:

Security Question 1:

Security Answer 1:

Security Question 2:

Security Answer 2:

Notes:

Website:

Username: | Email:

Password:

Security Question 1:

Security Answer 1:

Security Question 2:

Security Answer 2:

Notes:

Website:

Username: | Email:

Password:

Security Question 1:

Security Answer 1:

Security Question 2:

Security Answer 2:

Notes:

Website:

Username: | Email:

Password:

Security Question 1:

Security Answer 1:

Security Question 2:

Security Answer 2:

Notes:

Website:

Username: Email:

Password:

Security Question 1:

Security Answer 1:

Security Question 2:

Security Answer 2:

Notes:

Website:

Username: Email:

Password:

Security Question 1:

Security Answer 1:

Security Question 2:

Security Answer 2:

Notes:

Website:

Username: Email:

Password:

Security Question 1:

Security Answer 1:

Security Question 2:

Security Answer 2:

Notes:

Website:

Username: Email:

Password:

Security Question 1:

Security Answer 1:

Security Question 2:

Security Answer 2:

Notes:

Website:

Username: Email:

Password:

Security Question 1:

Security Answer 1:

Security Question 2:

Security Answer 2:

Notes:

Website:

Username: Email:

Password:

Security Question 1:

Security Answer 1:

Security Question 2:

Security Answer 2:

Notes:

Username: Email:

Password:

Security Question 1:

Security Answer 1:

Security Question 2:

Security Answer 2:

Notes:

Username: Email:

Password:

Security Question 1:

Security Answer 1:

Security Question 2:

Security Answer 2:

Notes:

Username: Email:

Password:

Security Question 1:

Security Answer 1:

Security Question 2:

Security Answer 2:

Notes:

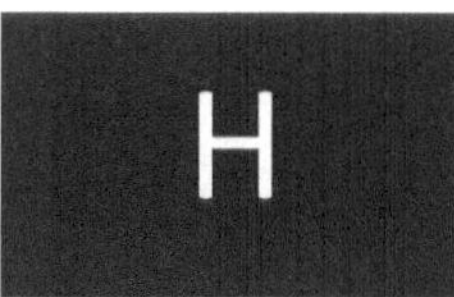

Website:

Username: Email:

Password:

Security Question 1:

Security Answer 1:

Security Question 2:

Security Answer 2:

Notes:

Website:

Username: Email:

Password:

Security Question 1:

Security Answer 1:

Security Question 2:

Security Answer 2:

Notes:

Website:

Username: Email:

Password:

Security Question 1:

Security Answer 1:

Security Question 2:

Security Answer 2:

Notes:

Username: Email:

Password:

Security Question 1:

Security Answer 1:

Security Question 2:

Security Answer 2:

Notes:

Website:

Username: Email:

Password:

Security Question 1:

Security Answer 1:

Security Question 2:

Security Answer 2:

Notes:

Website:

Username: Email:

Password:

Security Question 1:

Security Answer 1:

Security Question 2:

Security Answer 2:

Notes:

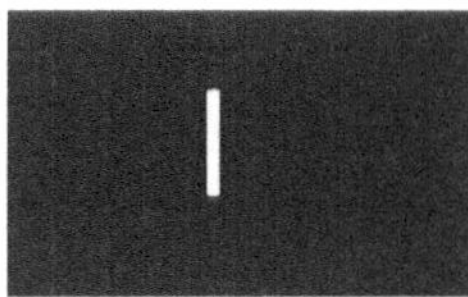

Website:

Username: Email:

Password:

Security Question 1:

Security Answer 1:

Security Question 2:

Security Answer 2:

Notes:

Website:

Username: Email:

Password:

Security Question 1:

Security Answer 1:

Security Question 2:

Security Answer 2:

Notes:

Website:

Username: Email:

Password:

Security Question 1:

Security Answer 1:

Security Question 2:

Security Answer 2:

Notes:

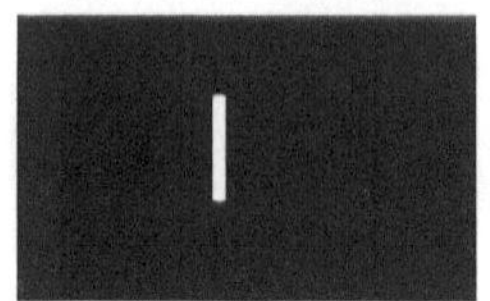

Website:

Username: Email:

Password:

Security Question 1:

Security Answer 1:

Security Question 2:

Security Answer 2:

Notes:

Website:

Username: Email:

Password:

Security Question 1:

Security Answer 1:

Security Question 2:

Security Answer 2:

Notes:

Website:

Username: Email:

Password:

Security Question 1:

Security Answer 1:

Security Question 2:

Security Answer 2:

Notes:

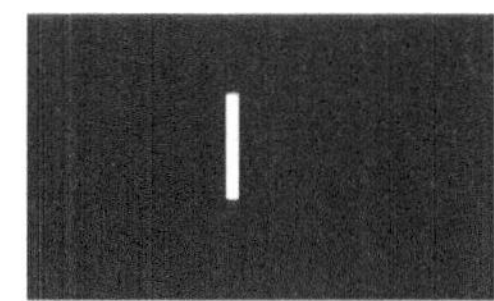

Website:

Username: Email:

Password:

Security Question 1:

Security Answer 1:

Security Question 2:

Security Answer 2:

Notes:

Website:

Username: Email:

Password:

Security Question 1:

Security Answer 1:

Security Question 2:

Security Answer 2:

Notes:

Website:

Username: Email:

Password:

Security Question 1:

Security Answer 1:

Security Question 2:

Security Answer 2:

Notes:

Website:

Username:	Email:

Password:

Security Question 1:

Security Answer 1:

Security Question 2:

Security Answer 2:

Notes:

Website:

Username:	Email:

Password:

Security Question 1:

Security Answer 1:

Security Question 2:

Security Answer 2:

Notes:

Website:

Username:	Email:

Password:

Security Question 1:

Security Answer 1:

Security Question 2:

Security Answer 2:

Notes:

Website:

Username: Email:

Password:

Security Question 1:

Security Answer 1:

Security Question 2:

Security Answer 2:

Notes:

Website:

Username: Email:

Password:

Security Question 1:

Security Answer 1:

Security Question 2:

Security Answer 2:

Notes:

Website:

Username: Email:

Password:

Security Question 1:

Security Answer 1:

Security Question 2:

Security Answer 2:

Notes:

Website:

Username: Email:

Password:

Security Question 1:

Security Answer 1:

Security Question 2:

Security Answer 2:

Notes:

Website:

Username: Email:

Password:

Security Question 1:

Security Answer 1:

Security Question 2:

Security Answer 2:

Notes:

Website:

Username: Email:

Password:

Security Question 1:

Security Answer 1:

Security Question 2:

Security Answer 2:

Notes:

J

Website:

Username: Email:

Password:

Security Question 1:

Security Answer 1:

Security Question 2:

Security Answer 2:

Notes:

Website:

Username: Email:

Password:

Security Question 1:

Security Answer 1:

Security Question 2:

Security Answer 2:

Notes:

Website:

Username: Email:

Password:

Security Question 1:

Security Answer 1:

Security Question 2:

Security Answer 2:

Notes:

Website:

Username: Email:

Password:

Security Question 1:

Security Answer 1:

Security Question 2:

Security Answer 2:

Notes:

Website:

Username: Email:

Password:

Security Question 1:

Security Answer 1:

Security Question 2:

Security Answer 2:

Notes:

Website:

Username: Email:

Password:

Security Question 1:

Security Answer 1:

Security Question 2:

Security Answer 2:

Notes:

Website:

Username: Email:

Password:

Security Question 1:

Security Answer 1:

Security Question 2:

Security Answer 2:

Notes:

Website:

Username: Email:

Password:

Security Question 1:

Security Answer 1:

Security Question 2:

Security Answer 2:

Notes:

Website:

Username: Email:

Password:

Security Question 1:

Security Answer 1:

Security Question 2:

Security Answer 2:

Notes:

J

Username: Email:

Password:

Security Question 1:

Security Answer 1:

Security Question 2:

Security Answer 2:

Notes:

Website:

Username: Email:

Password:

Security Question 1:

Security Answer 1:

Security Question 2:

Security Answer 2:

Notes:

Website:

Username: Email:

Password:

Security Question 1:

Security Answer 1:

Security Question 2:

Security Answer 2:

Notes:

Website:

Username: Email:

Password:

Security Question 1:

Security Answer 1:

Security Question 2:

Security Answer 2:

Notes:

Website:

Username: Email:

Password:

Security Question 1:

Security Answer 1:

Security Question 2:

Security Answer 2:

Notes:

Website:

Username: Email:

Password:

Security Question 1:

Security Answer 1:

Security Question 2:

Security Answer 2:

Notes:

Website:

Username: | Email:

Password:

Security Question 1:

Security Answer 1:

Security Question 2:

Security Answer 2:

Notes:

Website:

Username: | Email:

Password:

Security Question 1:

Security Answer 1:

Security Question 2:

Security Answer 2:

Notes:

Website:

Username: | Email:

Password:

Security Question 1:

Security Answer 1:

Security Question 2:

Security Answer 2:

Notes:

Website:

Username: Email:

Password:

Security Question 1:

Security Answer 1:

Security Question 2:

Security Answer 2:

Notes:

Website:

Username: Email:

Password:

Security Question 1:

Security Answer 1:

Security Question 2:

Security Answer 2:

Notes:

Website:

Username: Email:

Password:

Security Question 1:

Security Answer 1:

Security Question 2:

Security Answer 2:

Notes:

Website:

Username: Email:

Password:

Security Question 1:

Security Answer 1:

Security Question 2:

Security Answer 2:

Notes:

Website:

Username: Email:

Password:

Security Question 1:

Security Answer 1:

Security Question 2:

Security Answer 2:

Notes:

Website:

Username: Email:

Password:

Security Question 1:

Security Answer 1:

Security Question 2:

Security Answer 2:

Notes:

Website:

Username: Email:

Password:

Security Question 1:

Security Answer 1:

Security Question 2:

Security Answer 2:

Notes:

Website:

Username: Email:

Password:

Security Question 1:

Security Answer 1:

Security Question 2:

Security Answer 2:

Notes:

Website:

Username: Email:

Password:

Security Question 1:

Security Answer 1:

Security Question 2:

Security Answer 2:

Notes:

Website:

Username: Email:

Password:

Security Question 1:

Security Answer 1:

Security Question 2:

Security Answer 2:

Notes:

Website:

Username: Email:

Password:

Security Question 1:

Security Answer 1:

Security Question 2:

Security Answer 2:

Notes:

Website:

Username: Email:

Password:

Security Question 1:

Security Answer 1:

Security Question 2:

Security Answer 2:

Notes:

Website:

Username: | Email:

Password:

Security Question 1:

Security Answer 1:

Security Question 2:

Security Answer 2:

Notes:

Website:

Username: | Email:

Password:

Security Question 1:

Security Answer 1:

Security Question 2:

Security Answer 2:

Notes:

Website:

Username: | Email:

Password:

Security Question 1:

Security Answer 1:

Security Question 2:

Security Answer 2:

Notes:

Website:

Username: Email:

Password:

Security Question 1:

Security Answer 1:

Security Question 2:

Security Answer 2:

Notes:

Website:

Username: Email:

Password:

Security Question 1:

Security Answer 1:

Security Question 2:

Security Answer 2:

Notes:

Website:

Username: Email:

Password:

Security Question 1:

Security Answer 1:

Security Question 2:

Security Answer 2:

Notes:

Website:

Username: Email:

Password:

Security Question 1:

Security Answer 1:

Security Question 2:

Security Answer 2:

Notes:

Website:

Username: Email:

Password:

Security Question 1:

Security Answer 1:

Security Question 2:

Security Answer 2:

Notes:

Website:

Username: Email:

Password:

Security Question 1:

Security Answer 1:

Security Question 2:

Security Answer 2:

Notes:

Website:

Username: Email:

Password:

Security Question 1:

Security Answer 1:

Security Question 2:

Security Answer 2:

Notes:

Website:

Username: Email:

Password:

Security Question 1:

Security Answer 1:

Security Question 2:

Security Answer 2:

Notes:

Website:

Username: Email:

Password:

Security Question 1:

Security Answer 1:

Security Question 2:

Security Answer 2:

Notes:

Website:

Username: Email:

Password:

Security Question 1:

Security Answer 1:

Security Question 2:

Security Answer 2:

Notes:

Website:

Username: Email:

Password:

Security Question 1:

Security Answer 1:

Security Question 2:

Security Answer 2:

Notes:

Website:

Username: Email:

Password:

Security Question 1:

Security Answer 1:

Security Question 2:

Security Answer 2:

Notes:

L

Website:

Username: Email:

Password:

Security Question 1:

Security Answer 1:

Security Question 2:

Security Answer 2:

Notes:

Website:

Username: Email:

Password:

Security Question 1:

Security Answer 1:

Security Question 2:

Security Answer 2:

Notes:

Website:

Username: Email:

Password:

Security Question 1:

Security Answer 1:

Security Question 2:

Security Answer 2:

Notes:

Website:

Username: Email:

Password:

Security Question 1:

Security Answer 1:

Security Question 2:

Security Answer 2:

Notes:

Website:

Username: Email:

Password:

Security Question 1:

Security Answer 1:

Security Question 2:

Security Answer 2:

Notes:

Website:

Username: Email:

Password:

Security Question 1:

Security Answer 1:

Security Question 2:

Security Answer 2:

Notes:

Website:	
Username:	Email:
Password:	
Security Question 1:	
Security Answer 1:	
Security Question 2:	
Security Answer 2:	
Notes:	

Website:	
Username:	Email:
Password:	
Security Question 1:	
Security Answer 1:	
Security Question 2:	
Security Answer 2:	
Notes:	

Website:	
Username:	Email:
Password:	
Security Question 1:	
Security Answer 1:	
Security Question 2:	
Security Answer 2:	
Notes:	

Website:

Username: ____________ Email: ____________

Password:

Security Question 1:

Security Answer 1:

Security Question 2:

Security Answer 2:

Notes:

Website:

Username: ____________ Email: ____________

Password:

Security Question 1:

Security Answer 1:

Security Question 2:

Security Answer 2:

Notes:

Website:

Username: ____________ Email: ____________

Password:

Security Question 1:

Security Answer 1:

Security Question 2:

Security Answer 2:

Notes:

Website:

Username: Email:

Password:

Security Question 1:

Security Answer 1:

Security Question 2:

Security Answer 2:

Notes:

Website:

Username: Email:

Password:

Security Question 1:

Security Answer 1:

Security Question 2:

Security Answer 2:

Notes:

Website:

Username: Email:

Password:

Security Question 1:

Security Answer 1:

Security Question 2:

Security Answer 2:

Notes:

Website:

Username: Email:

Password:

Security Question 1:

Security Answer 1:

Security Question 2:

Security Answer 2:

Notes:

Website:

Username: Email:

Password:

Security Question 1:

Security Answer 1:

Security Question 2:

Security Answer 2:

Notes:

Website:

Username: Email:

Password:

Security Question 1:

Security Answer 1:

Security Question 2:

Security Answer 2:

Notes:

Website:

Username: Email:

Password:

Security Question 1:

Security Answer 1:

Security Question 2:

Security Answer 2:

Notes:

Website:

Username: Email:

Password:

Security Question 1:

Security Answer 1:

Security Question 2:

Security Answer 2:

Notes:

Website:

Username: Email:

Password:

Security Question 1:

Security Answer 1:

Security Question 2:

Security Answer 2:

Notes:

Website:

Username: Email:

Password:

Security Question 1:

Security Answer 1:

Security Question 2:

Security Answer 2:

Notes:

Website:

Username: Email:

Password:

Security Question 1:

Security Answer 1:

Security Question 2:

Security Answer 2:

Notes:

Website:

Username: Email:

Password:

Security Question 1:

Security Answer 1:

Security Question 2:

Security Answer 2:

Notes:

Website:

Username: Email:

Password:

Security Question 1:

Security Answer 1:

Security Question 2:

Security Answer 2:

Notes:

Website:

Username: Email:

Password:

Security Question 1:

Security Answer 1:

Security Question 2:

Security Answer 2:

Notes:

Website:

Username: Email:

Password:

Security Question 1:

Security Answer 1:

Security Question 2:

Security Answer 2:

Notes:

Website:

Username: Email:

Password:

Security Question 1:

Security Answer 1:

Security Question 2:

Security Answer 2:

Notes:

Website:

Username: Email:

Password:

Security Question 1:

Security Answer 1:

Security Question 2:

Security Answer 2:

Notes:

Website:

Username: Email:

Password:

Security Question 1:

Security Answer 1:

Security Question 2:

Security Answer 2:

Notes:

Website:

Username: Email:

Password:

Security Question 1:

Security Answer 1:

Security Question 2:

Security Answer 2:

Notes:

Website:

Username: Email:

Password:

Security Question 1:

Security Answer 1:

Security Question 2:

Security Answer 2:

Notes:

Website:

Username: Email:

Password:

Security Question 1:

Security Answer 1:

Security Question 2:

Security Answer 2:

Notes:

N

Website:

Username: Email:

Password:

Security Question 1:

Security Answer 1:

Security Question 2:

Security Answer 2:

Notes:

Website:

Username: Email:

Password:

Security Question 1:

Security Answer 1:

Security Question 2:

Security Answer 2:

Notes:

Website:

Username: Email:

Password:

Security Question 1:

Security Answer 1:

Security Question 2:

Security Answer 2:

Notes:

Website:

Username: Email:

Password:

Security Question 1:

Security Answer 1:

Security Question 2:

Security Answer 2:

Notes:

Website:

Username: Email:

Password:

Security Question 1:

Security Answer 1:

Security Question 2:

Security Answer 2:

Notes:

Website:

Username: Email:

Password:

Security Question 1:

Security Answer 1:

Security Question 2:

Security Answer 2:

Notes:

N

Website:

Username: Email:

Password:

Security Question 1:

Security Answer 1:

Security Question 2:

Security Answer 2:

Notes:

Website:

Username: Email:

Password:

Security Question 1:

Security Answer 1:

Security Question 2:

Security Answer 2:

Notes:

Website:

Username: Email:

Password:

Security Question 1:

Security Answer 1:

Security Question 2:

Security Answer 2:

Notes:

Website:

Username: Email:

Password:

Security Question 1:

Security Answer 1:

Security Question 2:

Security Answer 2:

Notes:

Website:

Username: Email:

Password:

Security Question 1:

Security Answer 1:

Security Question 2:

Security Answer 2:

Notes:

Website:

Username: Email:

Password:

Security Question 1:

Security Answer 1:

Security Question 2:

Security Answer 2:

Notes:

Website:

Username: Email:

Password:

Security Question 1:

Security Answer 1:

Security Question 2:

Security Answer 2:

Notes:

Website:

Username: Email:

Password:

Security Question 1:

Security Answer 1:

Security Question 2:

Security Answer 2:

Notes:

Website:

Username: Email:

Password:

Security Question 1:

Security Answer 1:

Security Question 2:

Security Answer 2:

Notes:

Website:

Username: Email:

Password:

Security Question 1:

Security Answer 1:

Security Question 2:

Security Answer 2:

Notes:

Website:

Username: Email:

Password:

Security Question 1:

Security Answer 1:

Security Question 2:

Security Answer 2:

Notes:

Website:

Username: Email:

Password:

Security Question 1:

Security Answer 1:

Security Question 2:

Security Answer 2:

Notes:

Website:

Username: Email:

Password:

Security Question 1:

Security Answer 1:

Security Question 2:

Security Answer 2:

Notes:

Website:

Username: Email:

Password:

Security Question 1:

Security Answer 1:

Security Question 2:

Security Answer 2:

Notes:

Website:

Username: Email:

Password:

Security Question 1:

Security Answer 1:

Security Question 2:

Security Answer 2:

Notes:

Website:

Username: Email:

Password:

Security Question 1:

Security Answer 1:

Security Question 2:

Security Answer 2:

Notes:

Website:

Username: Email:

Password:

Security Question 1:

Security Answer 1:

Security Question 2:

Security Answer 2:

Notes:

Website:

Username: Email:

Password:

Security Question 1:

Security Answer 1:

Security Question 2:

Security Answer 2:

Notes:

Website:

Username: Email:

Password:

Security Question 1:

Security Answer 1:

Security Question 2:

Security Answer 2:

Notes:

Website:

Username: Email:

Password:

Security Question 1:

Security Answer 1:

Security Question 2:

Security Answer 2:

Notes:

Website:

Username: Email:

Password:

Security Question 1:

Security Answer 1:

Security Question 2:

Security Answer 2:

Notes:

Username: Email:

Password:

Security Question 1:

Security Answer 1:

Security Question 2:

Security Answer 2:

Notes:

Website:

Username: Email:

Password:

Security Question 1:

Security Answer 1:

Security Question 2:

Security Answer 2:

Notes:

Website:

Username: Email:

Password:

Security Question 1:

Security Answer 1:

Security Question 2:

Security Answer 2:

Notes:

P

Website:

Username: Email:

Password:

Security Question 1:

Security Answer 1:

Security Question 2:

Security Answer 2:

Notes:

Website:

Username: Email:

Password:

Security Question 1:

Security Answer 1:

Security Question 2:

Security Answer 2:

Notes:

Website:

Username: Email:

Password:

Security Question 1:

Security Answer 1:

Security Question 2:

Security Answer 2:

Notes:

Website:

Username: Email:

Password:

Security Question 1:

Security Answer 1:

Security Question 2:

Security Answer 2:

Notes:

Website:

Username: Email:

Password:

Security Question 1:

Security Answer 1:

Security Question 2:

Security Answer 2:

Notes:

Website:

Username: Email:

Password:

Security Question 1:

Security Answer 1:

Security Question 2:

Security Answer 2:

Notes:

P

Website:

Username: Email:

Password:

Security Question 1:

Security Answer 1:

Security Question 2:

Security Answer 2:

Notes:

Website:

Username: Email:

Password:

Security Question 1:

Security Answer 1:

Security Question 2:

Security Answer 2:

Notes:

Website:

Username: Email:

Password:

Security Question 1:

Security Answer 1:

Security Question 2:

Security Answer 2:

Notes:

Website:

Username: Email:

Password:

Security Question 1:

Security Answer 1:

Security Question 2:

Security Answer 2:

Notes:

Website:

Username: Email:

Password:

Security Question 1:

Security Answer 1:

Security Question 2:

Security Answer 2:

Notes:

Website:

Username: Email:

Password:

Security Question 1:

Security Answer 1:

Security Question 2:

Security Answer 2:

Notes:

P

Website:

Username: Email:

Password:

Security Question 1:

Security Answer 1:

Security Question 2:

Security Answer 2:

Notes:

Website:

Username: Email:

Password:

Security Question 1:

Security Answer 1:

Security Question 2:

Security Answer 2:

Notes:

Website:

Username: Email:

Password:

Security Question 1:

Security Answer 1:

Security Question 2:

Security Answer 2:

Notes:

Q

Website:

Username: Email:

Password:

Security Question 1:

Security Answer 1:

Security Question 2:

Security Answer 2:

Notes:

Website:

Username: Email:

Password:

Security Question 1:

Security Answer 1:

Security Question 2:

Security Answer 2:

Notes:

Website:

Username: Email:

Password:

Security Question 1:

Security Answer 1:

Security Question 2:

Security Answer 2:

Notes:

Website:

Username: Email:

Password:

Security Question 1:

Security Answer 1:

Security Question 2:

Security Answer 2:

Notes:

Website:

Username: Email:

Password:

Security Question 1:

Security Answer 1:

Security Question 2:

Security Answer 2:

Notes:

Website:

Username: Email:

Password:

Security Question 1:

Security Answer 1:

Security Question 2:

Security Answer 2:

Notes:

Website:

Username: Email:

Password:

Security Question 1:

Security Answer 1:

Security Question 2:

Security Answer 2:

Notes:

Website:

Username: Email:

Password:

Security Question 1:

Security Answer 1:

Security Question 2:

Security Answer 2:

Notes:

Website:

Username: Email:

Password:

Security Question 1:

Security Answer 1:

Security Question 2:

Security Answer 2:

Notes:

Website:

Username: Email:

Password:

Security Question 1:

Security Answer 1:

Security Question 2:

Security Answer 2:

Notes:

Website:

Username: Email:

Password:

Security Question 1:

Security Answer 1:

Security Question 2:

Security Answer 2:

Notes:

Website:

Username: Email:

Password:

Security Question 1:

Security Answer 1:

Security Question 2:

Security Answer 2:

Notes:

Website:

Username: | Email:

Password:

Security Question 1:

Security Answer 1:

Security Question 2:

Security Answer 2:

Notes:

Website:

Username: | Email:

Password:

Security Question 1:

Security Answer 1:

Security Question 2:

Security Answer 2:

Notes:

Website:

Username: | Email:

Password:

Security Question 1:

Security Answer 1:

Security Question 2:

Security Answer 2:

Notes:

Website:

Username: Email:

Password:

Security Question 1:

Security Answer 1:

Security Question 2:

Security Answer 2:

Notes:

Website:

Username: Email:

Password:

Security Question 1:

Security Answer 1:

Security Question 2:

Security Answer 2:

Notes:

Website:

Username: Email:

Password:

Security Question 1:

Security Answer 1:

Security Question 2:

Security Answer 2:

Notes:

Website:

Username:	Email:

Password:

Security Question 1:

Security Answer 1:

Security Question 2:

Security Answer 2:

Notes:

Website:

Username:	Email:

Password:

Security Question 1:

Security Answer 1:

Security Question 2:

Security Answer 2:

Notes:

Website:

Username:	Email:

Password:

Security Question 1:

Security Answer 1:

Security Question 2:

Security Answer 2:

Notes:

Website:

Username: Email:

Password:

Security Question 1:

Security Answer 1:

Security Question 2:

Security Answer 2:

Notes:

Website:

Username: Email:

Password:

Security Question 1:

Security Answer 1:

Security Question 2:

Security Answer 2:

Notes:

Website:

Username: Email:

Password:

Security Question 1:

Security Answer 1:

Security Question 2:

Security Answer 2:

Notes:

Website:

Username: Email:

Password:

Security Question 1:

Security Answer 1:

Security Question 2:

Security Answer 2:

Notes:

Website:

Username: Email:

Password:

Security Question 1:

Security Answer 1:

Security Question 2:

Security Answer 2:

Notes:

Website:

Username: Email:

Password:

Security Question 1:

Security Answer 1:

Security Question 2:

Security Answer 2:

Notes:

Website:

Username: Email:

Password:

Security Question 1:

Security Answer 1:

Security Question 2:

Security Answer 2:

Notes:

Website:

Username: Email:

Password:

Security Question 1:

Security Answer 1:

Security Question 2:

Security Answer 2:

Notes:

Website:

Username: Email:

Password:

Security Question 1:

Security Answer 1:

Security Question 2:

Security Answer 2:

Notes:

Website:

Username: Email:

Password:

Security Question 1:

Security Answer 1:

Security Question 2:

Security Answer 2:

Notes:

Website:

Username: Email:

Password:

Security Question 1:

Security Answer 1:

Security Question 2:

Security Answer 2:

Notes:

Website:

Username: Email:

Password:

Security Question 1:

Security Answer 1:

Security Question 2:

Security Answer 2:

Notes:

Website:

Username: Email:

Password:

Security Question 1:

Security Answer 1:

Security Question 2:

Security Answer 2:

Notes:

Website:

Username: Email:

Password:

Security Question 1:

Security Answer 1:

Security Question 2:

Security Answer 2:

Notes:

Website:

Username: Email:

Password:

Security Question 1:

Security Answer 1:

Security Question 2:

Security Answer 2:

Notes:

S

Website:

Username: | Email:

Password:

Security Question 1:

Security Answer 1:

Security Question 2:

Security Answer 2:

Notes:

Website:

Username: | Email:

Password:

Security Question 1:

Security Answer 1:

Security Question 2:

Security Answer 2:

Notes:

Website:

Username: | Email:

Password:

Security Question 1:

Security Answer 1:

Security Question 2:

Security Answer 2:

Notes:

S

Website:

Username: Email:

Password:

Security Question 1:

Security Answer 1:

Security Question 2:

Security Answer 2:

Notes:

Website:

Username: Email:

Password:

Security Question 1:

Security Answer 1:

Security Question 2:

Security Answer 2:

Notes:

Website:

Username: Email:

Password:

Security Question 1:

Security Answer 1:

Security Question 2:

Security Answer 2:

Notes:

S

Website:

Username: Email:

Password:

Security Question 1:

Security Answer 1:

Security Question 2:

Security Answer 2:

Notes:

Website:

Username: Email:

Password:

Security Question 1:

Security Answer 1:

Security Question 2:

Security Answer 2:

Notes:

Website:

Username: Email:

Password:

Security Question 1:

Security Answer 1:

Security Question 2:

Security Answer 2:

Notes:

S

Website:

Username: | Email:

Password:

Security Question 1:

Security Answer 1:

Security Question 2:

Security Answer 2:

Notes:

Website:

Username: | Email:

Password:

Security Question 1:

Security Answer 1:

Security Question 2:

Security Answer 2:

Notes:

Website:

Username: | Email:

Password:

Security Question 1:

Security Answer 1:

Security Question 2:

Security Answer 2:

Notes:

S

Website:

Username: | Email:

Password:

Security Question 1:

Security Answer 1:

Security Question 2:

Security Answer 2:

Notes:

Website:

Username: | Email:

Password:

Security Question 1:

Security Answer 1:

Security Question 2:

Security Answer 2:

Notes:

Website:

Username: | Email:

Password:

Security Question 1:

Security Answer 1:

Security Question 2:

Security Answer 2:

Notes:

S

Website:

Username: Email:

Password:

Security Question 1:

Security Answer 1:

Security Question 2:

Security Answer 2:

Notes:

Website:

Username: Email:

Password:

Security Question 1:

Security Answer 1:

Security Question 2:

Security Answer 2:

Notes:

Website:

Username: Email:

Password:

Security Question 1:

Security Answer 1:

Security Question 2:

Security Answer 2:

Notes:

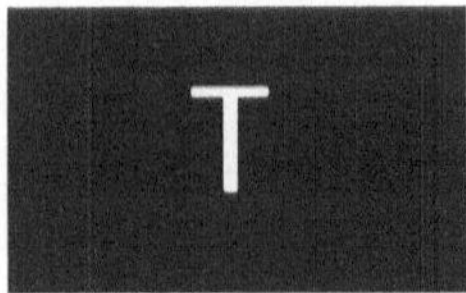

Website:

Username: Email:

Password:

Security Question 1:

Security Answer 1:

Security Question 2:

Security Answer 2:

Notes:

Website:

Username: Email:

Password:

Security Question 1:

Security Answer 1:

Security Question 2:

Security Answer 2:

Notes:

Website:

Username: Email:

Password:

Security Question 1:

Security Answer 1:

Security Question 2:

Security Answer 2:

Notes:

Website:

Username: Email:

Password:

Security Question 1:

Security Answer 1:

Security Question 2:

Security Answer 2:

Notes:

Website:

Username: Email:

Password:

Security Question 1:

Security Answer 1:

Security Question 2:

Security Answer 2:

Notes:

Website:

Username: Email:

Password:

Security Question 1:

Security Answer 1:

Security Question 2:

Security Answer 2:

Notes:

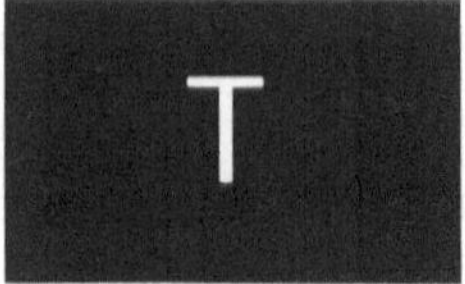

Website:

Username: Email:

Password:

Security Question 1:

Security Answer 1:

Security Question 2:

Security Answer 2:

Notes:

Website:

Username: Email:

Password:

Security Question 1:

Security Answer 1:

Security Question 2:

Security Answer 2:

Notes:

Website:

Username: Email:

Password:

Security Question 1:

Security Answer 1:

Security Question 2:

Security Answer 2:

Notes:

T

Website:

Username: Email:

Password:

Security Question 1:

Security Answer 1:

Security Question 2:

Security Answer 2:

Notes:

Website:

Username: Email:

Password:

Security Question 1:

Security Answer 1:

Security Question 2:

Security Answer 2:

Notes:

Website:

Username: Email:

Password:

Security Question 1:

Security Answer 1:

Security Question 2:

Security Answer 2:

Notes:

Website:

Username: Email:

Password:

Security Question 1:

Security Answer 1:

Security Question 2:

Security Answer 2:

Notes:

Website:

Username: Email:

Password:

Security Question 1:

Security Answer 1:

Security Question 2:

Security Answer 2:

Notes:

Website:

Username: Email:

Password:

Security Question 1:

Security Answer 1:

Security Question 2:

Security Answer 2:

Notes:

Website:

Username: Email:

Password:

Security Question 1:

Security Answer 1:

Security Question 2:

Security Answer 2:

Notes:

Website:

Username: Email:

Password:

Security Question 1:

Security Answer 1:

Security Question 2:

Security Answer 2:

Notes:

Website:

Username: Email:

Password:

Security Question 1:

Security Answer 1:

Security Question 2:

Security Answer 2:

Notes:

Website:

Username: Email:

Password:

Security Question 1:

Security Answer 1:

Security Question 2:

Security Answer 2:

Notes:

Website:

Username: Email:

Password:

Security Question 1:

Security Answer 1:

Security Question 2:

Security Answer 2:

Notes:

Website:

Username: Email:

Password:

Security Question 1:

Security Answer 1:

Security Question 2:

Security Answer 2:

Notes:

Website:

Username: Email:

Password:

Security Question 1:

Security Answer 1:

Security Question 2:

Security Answer 2:

Notes:

Website:

Username: Email:

Password:

Security Question 1:

Security Answer 1:

Security Question 2:

Security Answer 2:

Notes:

Website:

Username: Email:

Password:

Security Question 1:

Security Answer 1:

Security Question 2:

Security Answer 2:

Notes:

Website:

Username: Email:

Password:

Security Question 1:

Security Answer 1:

Security Question 2:

Security Answer 2:

Notes:

Website:

Username: Email:

Password:

Security Question 1:

Security Answer 1:

Security Question 2:

Security Answer 2:

Notes:

Website:

Username: Email:

Password:

Security Question 1:

Security Answer 1:

Security Question 2:

Security Answer 2:

Notes:

Website:

Username: Email:

Password:

Security Question 1:

Security Answer 1:

Security Question 2:

Security Answer 2:

Notes:

Website:

Username: Email:

Password:

Security Question 1:

Security Answer 1:

Security Question 2:

Security Answer 2:

Notes:

Website:

Username: Email:

Password:

Security Question 1:

Security Answer 1:

Security Question 2:

Security Answer 2:

Notes:

Website:	
Username:	Email:
Password:	
Security Question 1:	
Security Answer 1:	
Security Question 2:	
Security Answer 2:	
Notes:	

Website:	
Username:	Email:
Password:	
Security Question 1:	
Security Answer 1:	
Security Question 2:	
Security Answer 2:	
Notes:	

Website:	
Username:	Email:
Password:	
Security Question 1:	
Security Answer 1:	
Security Question 2:	
Security Answer 2:	
Notes:	

Website:

Username: Email:

Password:

Security Question 1:

Security Answer 1:

Security Question 2:

Security Answer 2:

Notes:

Website:

Username: Email:

Password:

Security Question 1:

Security Answer 1:

Security Question 2:

Security Answer 2:

Notes:

Website:

Username: Email:

Password:

Security Question 1:

Security Answer 1:

Security Question 2:

Security Answer 2:

Notes:

Website:

Username: Email:

Password:

Security Question 1:

Security Answer 1:

Security Question 2:

Security Answer 2:

Notes:

Website:

Username: Email:

Password:

Security Question 1:

Security Answer 1:

Security Question 2:

Security Answer 2:

Notes:

Website:

Username: Email:

Password:

Security Question 1:

Security Answer 1:

Security Question 2:

Security Answer 2:

Notes:

Website:

Username: Email:

Password:

Security Question 1:

Security Answer 1:

Security Question 2:

Security Answer 2:

Notes:

Website:

Username: Email:

Password:

Security Question 1:

Security Answer 1:

Security Question 2:

Security Answer 2:

Notes:

Website:

Username: Email:

Password:

Security Question 1:

Security Answer 1:

Security Question 2:

Security Answer 2:

Notes:

Website:

Username: Email:

Password:

Security Question 1:

Security Answer 1:

Security Question 2:

Security Answer 2:

Notes:

Website:

Username: Email:

Password:

Security Question 1:

Security Answer 1:

Security Question 2:

Security Answer 2:

Notes:

Website:

Username: Email:

Password:

Security Question 1:

Security Answer 1:

Security Question 2:

Security Answer 2:

Notes:

Website:

Username: Email:

Password:

Security Question 1:

Security Answer 1:

Security Question 2:

Security Answer 2:

Notes:

Website:

Username: Email:

Password:

Security Question 1:

Security Answer 1:

Security Question 2:

Security Answer 2:

Notes:

Website:

Username: Email:

Password:

Security Question 1:

Security Answer 1:

Security Question 2:

Security Answer 2:

Notes:

Website:

Username: Email:

Password:

Security Question 1:

Security Answer 1:

Security Question 2:

Security Answer 2:

Notes:

Website:

Username: Email:

Password:

Security Question 1:

Security Answer 1:

Security Question 2:

Security Answer 2:

Notes:

Website:

Username: Email:

Password:

Security Question 1:

Security Answer 1:

Security Question 2:

Security Answer 2:

Notes:

Website:

Username: | Email:

Password:

Security Question 1:

Security Answer 1:

Security Question 2:

Security Answer 2:

Notes:

Website:

Username: | Email:

Password:

Security Question 1:

Security Answer 1:

Security Question 2:

Security Answer 2:

Notes:

Website:

Username: | Email:

Password:

Security Question 1:

Security Answer 1:

Security Question 2:

Security Answer 2:

Notes:

Website:	
Username:	Email:
Password:	
Security Question 1:	
Security Answer 1:	
Security Question 2:	
Security Answer 2:	
Notes:	

Website:	
Username:	Email:
Password:	
Security Question 1:	
Security Answer 1:	
Security Question 2:	
Security Answer 2:	
Notes:	

Website:	
Username:	Email:
Password:	
Security Question 1:	
Security Answer 1:	
Security Question 2:	
Security Answer 2:	
Notes:	

Website:

Username: Email:

Password:

Security Question 1:

Security Answer 1:

Security Question 2:

Security Answer 2:

Notes:

Website:

Username: Email:

Password:

Security Question 1:

Security Answer 1:

Security Question 2:

Security Answer 2:

Notes:

Website:

Username: Email:

Password:

Security Question 1:

Security Answer 1:

Security Question 2:

Security Answer 2:

Notes:

Website:

Username: Email:

Password:

Security Question 1:

Security Answer 1:

Security Question 2:

Security Answer 2:

Notes:

Website:

Username: Email:

Password:

Security Question 1:

Security Answer 1:

Security Question 2:

Security Answer 2:

Notes:

Website:

Username: Email:

Password:

Security Question 1:

Security Answer 1:

Security Question 2:

Security Answer 2:

Notes:

Website:

Username: Email:

Password:

Security Question 1:

Security Answer 1:

Security Question 2:

Security Answer 2:

Notes:

Website:

Username: Email:

Password:

Security Question 1:

Security Answer 1:

Security Question 2:

Security Answer 2:

Notes:

Website:

Username: Email:

Password:

Security Question 1:

Security Answer 1:

Security Question 2:

Security Answer 2:

Notes:

Website:

Username: | Email:

Password:

Security Question 1:

Security Answer 1:

Security Question 2:

Security Answer 2:

Notes:

Website:

Username: | Email:

Password:

Security Question 1:

Security Answer 1:

Security Question 2:

Security Answer 2:

Notes:

Website:

Username: | Email:

Password:

Security Question 1:

Security Answer 1:

Security Question 2:

Security Answer 2:

Notes:

Website:

Username: Email:

Password:

Security Question 1:

Security Answer 1:

Security Question 2:

Security Answer 2:

Notes:

Website:

Username: Email:

Password:

Security Question 1:

Security Answer 1:

Security Question 2:

Security Answer 2:

Notes:

Website:

Username: Email:

Password:

Security Question 1:

Security Answer 1:

Security Question 2:

Security Answer 2:

Notes:

Website:	
Username:	Email:
Password:	
Security Question 1:	
Security Answer 1:	
Security Question 2:	
Security Answer 2:	
Notes:	

Website:	
Username:	Email:
Password:	
Security Question 1:	
Security Answer 1:	
Security Question 2:	
Security Answer 2:	
Notes:	

Website:	
Username:	Email:
Password:	
Security Question 1:	
Security Answer 1:	
Security Question 2:	
Security Answer 2:	
Notes:	

Website:

Username: Email:

Password:

Security Question 1:

Security Answer 1:

Security Question 2:

Security Answer 2:

Notes:

Website:

Username: Email:

Password:

Security Question 1:

Security Answer 1:

Security Question 2:

Security Answer 2:

Notes:

Website:

Username: Email:

Password:

Security Question 1:

Security Answer 1:

Security Question 2:

Security Answer 2:

Notes:

Website:

Username: Email:

Password:

Security Question 1:

Security Answer 1:

Security Question 2:

Security Answer 2:

Notes:

Website:

Username: Email:

Password:

Security Question 1:

Security Answer 1:

Security Question 2:

Security Answer 2:

Notes:

Website:

Username: Email:

Password:

Security Question 1:

Security Answer 1:

Security Question 2:

Security Answer 2:

Notes:

Website:

Username: Email:

Password:

Security Question 1:

Security Answer 1:

Security Question 2:

Security Answer 2:

Notes:

Website:

Username: Email:

Password:

Security Question 1:

Security Answer 1:

Security Question 2:

Security Answer 2:

Notes:

Website:

Username: Email:

Password:

Security Question 1:

Security Answer 1:

Security Question 2:

Security Answer 2:

Notes:

Website:	

Username: Email:

Password:

Security Question 1:

Security Answer 1:

Security Question 2:

Security Answer 2:

Notes:

Website:	

Username: Email:

Password:

Security Question 1:

Security Answer 1:

Security Question 2:

Security Answer 2:

Notes:

Website:	

Username: Email:

Password:

Security Question 1:

Security Answer 1:

Security Question 2:

Security Answer 2:

Notes:

Website:

Username: ___________________ Email: ___________________

Password:

Security Question 1:

Security Answer 1:

Security Question 2:

Security Answer 2:

Notes:

Website:

Username: ___________________ Email: ___________________

Password:

Security Question 1:

Security Answer 1:

Security Question 2:

Security Answer 2:

Notes:

Website:

Username: ___________________ Email: ___________________

Password:

Security Question 1:

Security Answer 1:

Security Question 2:

Security Answer 2:

Notes:

Website:

Username:	Email:

Password:

Security Question 1:

Security Answer 1:

Security Question 2:

Security Answer 2:

Notes:

Website:

Username:	Email:

Password:

Security Question 1:

Security Answer 1:

Security Question 2:

Security Answer 2:

Notes:

Website:

Username:	Email:

Password:

Security Question 1:

Security Answer 1:

Security Question 2:

Security Answer 2:

Notes:

Website:

Username: Email:

Password:

Security Question 1:

Security Answer 1:

Security Question 2:

Security Answer 2:

Notes:

Website:

Username: Email:

Password:

Security Question 1:

Security Answer 1:

Security Question 2:

Security Answer 2:

Notes:

Website:

Username: Email:

Password:

Security Question 1:

Security Answer 1:

Security Question 2:

Security Answer 2:

Notes:

Website:

Username: ___________________ Email: ___________________

Password:

Security Question 1:

Security Answer 1:

Security Question 2:

Security Answer 2:

Notes:

Website:

Username: ___________________ Email: ___________________

Password:

Security Question 1:

Security Answer 1:

Security Question 2:

Security Answer 2:

Notes:

Website:

Username: ___________________ Email: ___________________

Password:

Security Question 1:

Security Answer 1:

Security Question 2:

Security Answer 2:

Notes:

Website:

Username: Email:

Password:

Security Question 1:

Security Answer 1:

Security Question 2:

Security Answer 2:

Notes:

Website:

Username: Email:

Password:

Security Question 1:

Security Answer 1:

Security Question 2:

Security Answer 2:

Notes:

Website:

Username: Email:

Password:

Security Question 1:

Security Answer 1:

Security Question 2:

Security Answer 2:

Notes:

Website:

Username: Email:

Password:

Security Question 1:

Security Answer 1:

Security Question 2:

Security Answer 2:

Notes:

Website:

Username: Email:

Password:

Security Question 1:

Security Answer 1:

Security Question 2:

Security Answer 2:

Notes:

Website:

Username: Email:

Password:

Security Question 1:

Security Answer 1:

Security Question 2:

Security Answer 2:

Notes:

Website:

Username: Email:

Password:

Security Question 1:

Security Answer 1:

Security Question 2:

Security Answer 2:

Notes:

Website:

Username: Email:

Password:

Security Question 1:

Security Answer 1:

Security Question 2:

Security Answer 2:

Notes:

Website:

Username: Email:

Password:

Security Question 1:

Security Answer 1:

Security Question 2:

Security Answer 2:

Notes:

Z

Website:

Username: Email:

Password:

Security Question 1:

Security Answer 1:

Security Question 2:

Security Answer 2:

Notes:

Website:

Username: Email:

Password:

Security Question 1:

Security Answer 1:

Security Question 2:

Security Answer 2:

Notes:

Website:

Username: Email:

Password:

Security Question 1:

Security Answer 1:

Security Question 2:

Security Answer 2:

Notes:

Z

Website:

Username: Email:

Password:

Security Question 1:

Security Answer 1:

Security Question 2:

Security Answer 2:

Notes:

Website:

Username: Email:

Password:

Security Question 1:

Security Answer 1:

Security Question 2:

Security Answer 2:

Notes:

Website:

Username: Email:

Password:

Security Question 1:

Security Answer 1:

Security Question 2:

Security Answer 2:

Notes:

Z

Website:

Username: Email:

Password:

Security Question 1:

Security Answer 1:

Security Question 2:

Security Answer 2:

Notes:

Website:

Username: Email:

Password:

Security Question 1:

Security Answer 1:

Security Question 2:

Security Answer 2:

Notes:

Website:

Username: Email:

Password:

Security Question 1:

Security Answer 1:

Security Question 2:

Security Answer 2:

Notes:

Website:

Username: Email:

Password:

Security Question 1:

Security Answer 1:

Security Question 2:

Security Answer 2:

Notes:

Website:

Username: Email:

Password:

Security Question 1:

Security Answer 1:

Security Question 2:

Security Answer 2:

Notes:

Website:

Username: Email:

Password:

Security Question 1:

Security Answer 1:

Security Question 2:

Security Answer 2:

Notes:

Z

Website:

Username: Email:

Password:

Security Question 1:

Security Answer 1:

Security Question 2:

Security Answer 2:

Notes:

Website:

Username: Email:

Password:

Security Question 1:

Security Answer 1:

Security Question 2:

Security Answer 2:

Notes:

Website:

Username: Email:

Password:

Security Question 1:

Security Answer 1:

Security Question 2:

Security Answer 2:

Notes:

Z

Website:

Username: Email:

Password:

Security Question 1:

Security Answer 1:

Security Question 2:

Security Answer 2:

Notes:

Website:

Username: Email:

Password:

Security Question 1:

Security Answer 1:

Security Question 2:

Security Answer 2:

Notes:

Website:

Username: Email:

Password:

Security Question 1:

Security Answer 1:

Security Question 2:

Security Answer 2:

Notes:

www.ingramcontent.com/pod-product-compliance
Lightning Source LLC
Chambersburg PA
CBHW021404150726
47989CB00005B/2399